PHANTOM
CAPTAIN

THE OTTOLINE PRIZE

PUBLISHED IN THE UNITED STATES BY

FENCE BOOKS
36-09 28TH AVENUE, APT. 3R
ASTORIA, NY 11103-4518

WWW.FENCEPORTAL.ORG

THIS BOOK WAS PRINTED BY VERSA PRESS
DISTRIBUTED BY SMALL PRESS DISTRIBUTION
AND CONSORTIUM BOOK SALES AND DISTRIBUTION

COVER IMAGE IS A DETAIL OF "THE GARDEN SISTERS" BY SALLY ROSS
COLLECTION OF MARGUERITE STEED HOFFMAN
COVER AND INTERIOR DESIGN BY REBECCA WOLFF

LIBRARY OF CONGRESS CONTROL NUMBER: 2023946035
ISBN 13: 978-19443802-7-4

FIRST EDITION
10 9 8 7 6 5 4 3 2

PHANTOM CAPTAIN

kim rosenfield
the ottoline prize

FENCE BOOKS
ASTORIA NY

This captain has not only an infinite self-identity characteristic but, also, an infinite understanding. He has, furthermore, infinite sympathy with all captains of mechanisms similar to his. What is this UNDERSTANDING? It consists in an intuitive, non-graphable awareness of perfection, or of unity, or of eternity, or of infinity, or of truth....

R. BUCKMINSTER FULLER

'Fears' are as opaque as 'hopes.'
Is 'hope' different from desire?
Yes; like knots; it is desire + time
Or,

Desire + Frustration = Hopes ←—→ Fears.

W. R. BION

The sea is not less beautiful in our eyes because we know that sometimes ships are wrecked by it. On the contrary, this adds to its beauty.

SIMONE WEIL

For Nikolas

CONTENTS

I

LONGING CROSSES
THE SEA

There is a great deal to know about myself before I can start to see another. The metaphor of a sailboat helps me understand how I took in water in the form of pain even before my first breath, and by the time I finished grade school, my boat sat with tattered sails, low in the water, hull already full. I must try to release the water of the past

Every emotion is true
Every psychoanalytic fact
Accurately represented
When there is no further backward turn
And all political maneuvering
Has quietly come to an end

In this very identity
Sits a pleasurable condition
Void of wishes
Set in she/her position
As precious as a build-out
Of loneliness for two

Hushing-up tactics suffer greatly
under the burden of themselves
When you look at analysis
As a sort of Christmas present
Or a homeland of emotional life
Or a concern with the family constellation
Or genesis of illness
Which makes us all into astronauts

I keep talking to you myself, but I don't answer me so good

My aim in life is to expect others to conform to my particular ideals even if we all have trouble jumping the waves of hoops popping up. Therefore, I learned a new euphemism for an old obsession: "dropping kiddies at the pool." It functions like religion for people leading lives for whom those aims need to be able to come true

Keeping busy with regular routines is a coping mechanism for everybody who does not like us clowns who are actually not just joking

I'm hoping this book is remote from intrigue as I hate it when philosophers fall back on "affinity for the familiar" because the heartbreak becomes wider and sadder then

The best thing now would be for all associations to blow up

Here's my longing to be known and my fear of being known and the uncanny of not knowing and the ineffable experience of the limitless infinite and the unthought known and forms of not knowing and the dialectic interplay between discovery and avoidance and making myself known to others and being in the public eye versus the blank screen and the wish (need) to feel known or to remain unknown and unconscious knowing and the unknown core and the illusion of knowing and the role of values and cultural norms in shaping knowing and being known the mutual desire and fear in the room and the contested zone that demarks the boundaries between "me and you," "us and them," "I and not-I" and facts falsely represented as desires and desires falsely represented as facts and naming and locating inside and outside and myself and others and the collaborative intersubjective processes between subject and biographer and developmental accomplishments attained through gaining the capacity to recognize and face and bear lonely feelings and accepting and tolerating pain and frustration and intimacy and how many narratives interweave to express affects and intentions and goals of each member of the human race

This is your absolute last chance
to contact a very interesting man
who is on the precise same page as you

My changes are rapid enough to defy recognition.
There are those who expect me to function as anyone who attempts to be disguised as "a normal person." This is an *old possession* for people like me who realize how little anyone has learned from lessons constantly being served up by people who wish I had a more positive attitude. The conclusion is this:

a relationship ends when a person is reduced to serving as a kind of object

II

FORMER PRESENT TIMES

GOD I WISH I HAD A WIFE LIKE YOU

Everything is now an old story and much of my confusion is about how day and night split into parts by the motion of the universe. Everyone laughed at me as I tried to understand why it got dark at night and why light returned in the morning

I'm trying to deal with troubling matters as thoroughly feminist moments. Take the innocence of financial planners, whose only connections are, at best, in a manner, what might be regarded as impersonal. Whose expectations imply that accumulation of wealth is THE sole context through which activities that are awarded the utmost significance in our world are judged. The best example of this thinking is the idea:

Metaphors are investments instead of possessions

In conveying social relations and their incumbent responsibility on us, on our investment in weapons, on our wars against drugs, on over 6 million plus people in prisons right now, all of whom are being rationalized by just about everybody as steps that might be taken so that we can live in a world with an economy that is truly great, that breaks its own neck if anyone with instincts is allowed to try to defend themselves

Americans are terrible readers of anything as old and complex as a 1757 work on how sublime and beautiful changes upset our lives and became traumatic ideologies getting crowded out by a future like *Manners Maketh the Man*. We didn't fall for World War wit. Humor of the forbidden went on and on and we had to function with creative tensions that produced emotional intensity

My attitude should become more like my way of describing great observations. I need to know, from all the whatnot that gets in my way of thinking, about what is going on. That's when I'll finally have insight into what is bothering my characters

Word War wit is based on forbidden reciprocity that stands above political thinking's shoulders. "Peace without Victory" is lacking in triumphalism. Here I am thinking of war as a problem to be solved by not joining either side

I break the sword and am caught like a bunch of Baby Babylons meeting Gog and Magog for the first time as I line up for half an apocalypse f o r e v e r (if we even last that long)

I take a dim view of the last 100 years when parvenu leapfrog kept going in different directions and people scattered forever in a progressive emotional Nagasaki

I will never fight another war again as I would just get naked like when the most powerful earthquakes in my lifetime send puissant waves of water over our land

Institutions expand collective thinking to match the problems of individuals all the while expecting to make un-American activities involve eligible women in higher numbers. I am only betting on a casino of possibilities that this will become nothing different

What I thought I needed only an angel could provide though terror, disdain, and destroying me. The earth wants to say this in words, or in a Rodin sculpture: people will die not knowing what hit them. I tried to pick some lines from poems that wish you were here

Blurred self-image trump lifestyles by way of others rejecting me. I'm expected to continue this mockery of violence (promised by the state) as the best alternative to anarchy—like melted character-snowballs that end up in Hell in Paradise Lost. My subtext is now a world turned upside-down like an altar to an unknown God. Perfect for a culture like mine that would serve up hemlock to Socrates

Like Eve, who did not listen, matters got ponderous beyond what human appreciation understands even though I now have the right to describe anything that I want to as the muses keep feeding me. They make me curious about how people would react if I changed some punctuation, adjusted pauses between phrases, and didn't make the kind of sense that mere modern pauses might imply

The serpent throws fruit from the tree which Eve bites. Demons fall from heaven and I win the battle that sets the scene in Hell.

After that my head cannot help my brain keep up with everything and my thinking feels like angels escaping from fetters over a lake of fire. The best idea I can come up with for transporting despair is mixing Earth and Hell because everyone more or less finds themselves in Babylon in the end anyway where the Whore of Babylon lap-dances the beast and then raises a cup

Instead of having a culture smart enough to evaluate everything,
I rush into the cockpit in my snobbish dog outfit competing in a
popularity contest that is equal to my desire to mix Earth and Hell

Now our Beast of Babylon has whirligigs of light on top and can blast
a siren

I'm writing in despair along with others who renounce the tradition of
putting someone else as top dog in a global electronic situation where
social networks have no rules except to limit themselves to desires
of ego-bounding leader-treacle that signals more and more troubled
waters. My own interest is a form of escape from my own anarchy—
I'm a lifer at taking over low notes of culture

Sometimes the best parts of me float on my raft of metaphysical powers where I get overtones as bad as an augmented sixth. I'm familiar with what happens to people who are drunk, who are not supposed to slip into any kind of harmony. Bad things happen. In this America, where people are most comfortable inside their homes for most of the year, so much has fallen from its high horse that everybody starts combining their own songs, their own "Sympathy for the Devil." I am as American as suffering. Born from an epidemic of people who like to eat sugar for a high and make ineptitude fun, who are not yet social enough to understand pathological hatred is making history the wrong approach

I hardly ever smoke but man, reading Nietzsche takes me there! Like weird access to establishment death games which are one way of keeping score. I know I'm fighting when I actually have to stop to count the bodies as if war is a purification of what seems rotten when no one any longer has any great hopes in common. I'm a medically fictive personality, I want to die at the right time mentally. I'm also a happy person and happy people don't have big stories. This way social interactions become a real trick

THE POET IS ENDING THE RELATIONSHIP
BECAUSE OF LANGUAGE?

III

AESTHETICS OF THE INVISIBLE REALM

People who admire creative thinking are often unsure of what they are looking for or how long they will have to wait to get it. This book is about waiting in traffic. Kant, the ideal thinker, was always going nowhere, afraid of going somewhere and somewhere is a place in your heart. Kant could have gone to Berlin and been like anybody else but too many people want too many things and you can only manage to forget what's stuck in your own head

The idea of wanting disturbs people who understand this more as sad dis-enchantmentality. People get turned off when body counts become an escalation or when Nietzsche, a genius, sets words to music. I don't agree with anything I see or hear and my own interests are an appoggiatura to some form of escape from my own anarchy in which some heads get chopped off in the Klassics Klub and liberals become an endless string of Baby Babylons producing higher swindle for global electric piracy

Some people want a religion that grows, like an ossiferous grab-oxen, trying to maintain the role of fighting "Barbarians." Psalms are mentioned as opening guides to being mistreated. Religion as civil authority becomes a holy grail to the perfection of persecution and page 72 has a summary of how we become losers. Kierkegaard writes to an imaginary friend trying to describe how expectations provide eternal bliss when no authority could ever comprehend what people experience. When men with numbers get into bottlenecks they make pinwheels with cudgels then look like fools with disordered clothing

People expect tradition to continue in this world that shits and shuffles continuously and perhaps more so than ever might have a shock of recognition when I don't cry for their story. NOBODY wants more hermits, marmots, prairie dogs and woodchucks, like losers with superior wit motivated to penetrate what highly medicated brains of in-distinction dare not admit

Animal fat and fatty degeneracy make me more sensitive to Emanuel Swedenborg's description of chyle in the brain (having emulsified fat according to an unabridged dictionary). I never studied the lymph system but Swedenborg studied brains and found out how humans differ from animals and how the soul is far better off than most of us people

A world facing ruination surfs opportunities to discover what has never been said before:

If we can age, then life becomes a weird search for forgotten fruitcake.

Sometimes what we try to create is taken for vertiginous demands on older people who can never escape by taking more medicine and we are all older now.

Alles hat ein Ende
Aber eine Wurst
Hat zwei.

Everybody is too busy to question their own self-importance when governance by false promises is counted as usual. I've become suspicious of anyone who starts proclaiming: *Verily I have seen the Truth! Naked and barefoot to the neck!* Um, Literature—calling Captain Ahab! Giving readers an after-blast of hysteria or who the fink are you today? When my book is good it pictures philosophers as little boys declaring that the emperor hath no clothes. That's easy for me to say because in 1984 I thought I could get attention for the bare bones outline of a book on how to tear America limb from limb. I was also worried about getting a publisher if I had to find one myself

After a God Bless America political convention I got a large collection of rejection slips which Nietzsche cleverly avoided by having a publisher who could be paid to print what he was trying to say in book form even though I looked at the contents first to make sure this book skipped the c r a z y ideas of Zarathustra. Just try to drink that poison without getting any in your blood!

The creepy parts of this book remind me of taking a bus ride in middle America. The plot takes place so long ago that the characters try to keep from being sick by thinking about the bounce of physics they feel going from one place to another. Sometimes their bus goes to the mall, with stops at the airport, but it was not always easy to decide which ride was more like tree snakes slithering up in your bong water. I had so much to explore in ideas and in geography that I tried fixing silver iodide pictures in a salt solution when I had a physics lab . This required counting in the darkroom so I have a high functional level for learning. So much so that nobody likes me. When I published widely in 1984, it was the kind of thinking that dropped deep bombs. With, let's just say, some "room for failure"

Science for after-worlders or the grounds of intellect for dead European men is indexed with words that do not appear in my recently acquired unabridged dictionary. The book has hundreds of pages with section numbers making unusual topics clear to readers who are not versed in the science of living such as a definition of sordid avarice meaning: "expecting pleasure to fade as fast as an act ends, as in venereal love." It takes time to love money which is not natural for a superior mind as it is never natural but can only grow in the course of time as explained by the definition of animus on page 178. Death is the Big Decline but don't worry! On page 232 the soul lightens up!

Nietzsche called people who think the "Outer-Worlders." Kant was biting the hand that provided money for the ideas that produced his own work. Freud was treated as a product of an epistemology which served the kind of political economy the world is so stuck with today like frantic hacker whirligigers

Sometimes reading the same page at different times can help. Then I can re-imagine an excess of inwardness in which the incomprehensive and the unlimited and a little progression of more oppression drive the unconscious forward. This state runs the risk of becoming like a rock hut if felt for a very long time. If you haven't read this book then you're not a complete person because this book is heavy with people who keep trying to imagine the world solely as home to billions of shoppers and shoplifters we don't yet know. There is something great about freedom in a culture which allows so much to be going on when none of it fits together

I know that disinformation is a large part of any secret circus stunt. Where everything that happens at a circus is more convincing than in any part of the world that allegedly existed before events got summarized in this book, and people might be confused about anything anyone wrote before meta foreplay. This is only one set of confusions, LOL!! For suspense, people take interest in anyone trying to escape from their own ineptitude. But O my friend! There are no more friendly moves. Like, for example, if a female patient gets noticed by a soldier after the War and her mother freaks the fink out, who's left to figure out how to plead confusion?

IV

NATURE'S AFTERWORLD HOURS

When a kiss
is the hand
that guides
the child
let us not
go home
broken blossomed

Thunder strikes cascading shrapnel-blasted stems, shredding moldering roots into lactonic earth chum. Phenolic clouds convene like harpies overhead as spring breezes turn chill. Leather/woody/ amber thunder whips ozonated garden grounds in trespass of the tranquility of the day. A warm marble lion's head shatters into shards of mineralized pulverization in the stone courtyard. Milky tears of sotto voce helplessness tumble out of the sky soaking green earth, trying valiantly to nourish her. Lady Nature unleashes raspberry-tinged winds on tender and unsuspecting targets: Turkish (and maybe some Bulgarian but I doubt it) roses, as their young buds are rent, scattered in their sweet and jammy prime. This very cruel and very ruthless and very bad wind continues to torment the roses, flinging them about maniacally, like frankincense swung at vespers by delirious monks— bruising tender flesh, breaking tiny glands. Dear god, they are so mercilessly churned over and over. Suddenly, without warning, swift rapiers of lightning bombard the plum orchard, slashing dark fruit in two, singing overripe skin, ripping back raw flesh. Sticky nectar oozes into loamy earth, mixing with charred petals in somber mutating melancholy. In the long and sweeping dry-down, dirt-stained roots caress broken stems, wrap around mangled sister haws, lying as orangy-red corpses in nature's death grip of cultivar genocide. Cold raindrop after cold raindrop crush fragile anthers and fecund ovaries, snuffing out any memory of a once-perfect vegetal life. Hours later, a strange and unbidden musk creeps in with the first curl of dawn. The languid sun begins her spreadeagle rise across the forest floor. Silk- stockinged sinews of civet, patchouli, and ambroxan wrap fleshy legs around moist tips of rock hard roots and I orgasm all over myself with one swift spray

Here lies a list of surpluses and needs remaining:

Food
Meat

Who lives here?
I am
No
I am

You will show me how you came to be here
The memories are simple heroics

There is a much simpler memory—
The place where the sea meets the land

We have to shut ourselves off
We have to

It's proper to investigate
It's better not to know

Quench it. Quell it

Is our memory transmission
Still functioning?
We have lost our memory moments
No playback to proceeding images
No other memory in ages
To be shown without the consent
Of the individual

I will invoice our community
The community will follow my intuition—
Terribly exciting!

We can't equate my feelings
With yours
Its just entertainment
Again, these are key images:

My mother
My father

I am an artist
I do it with imagination
Fine genetic studies
Breaking DNA codes
Evolutionary changes

Every new hereditary disease
Broadens our imagination-spectrum
Emotional and psychotic elements
In relation to sociology

We are perfectly stabilized
The animal from the outside
Thinks of our equilibrium

Presence will dismay
Our tranquility
We are vulnerable
We know our lives are at stake
Otherwise we would rape and kill
(the disrupting effect—anything to relieve
our boredom)

I want to see more memories
A psychic disturbance
Avowal portends the future
How did we conjure up
A monster in our midst?

For?
Against?
Verdict?

Morning monster—time for work!

Whenever you're ready
Just ask me questions
Anything at all

I've got time
And plenty of it
21-hour days, 504 hours
30,240 minutes
one million 814,400 seconds

No retinal abnormalities
Discs and retinal vessels normal
No hemorrhages or vitriol leaking
Macular area clear

I am accused of transmitting
A negative aura
This is not so
I have studied our social
Emotional substructures for 54 years
My thoughts are constructive criticisms
I am innocent of psychic violence
We discuss it endlessly
Every little sin and misdemeanor
Racked over and over

I'll get six months at least
Prison?
No, aging

These sentences add up
They make you old
But they don't let you die

Final statement for the accused begins:
I confess to the charges
I try to suppress these thoughts
But they leak out at the second level

I think what I think
That's more like it

I hate you all
I hate you all
Especially me

V

IT'S BEEN AN ALMOST HYSTERICAL
TEST OF MY METTLE

I wanted to fend for myself
But couldn't even put one foot
Out the door

We tear at our wounds on Vita Instagram
When I slide
It is a deep dark
Hallucinogenic hole
A gourmet donut
Round how I've failed
At life at birth
At wisdom at hedging

I've ripped apart your life
Un-stoppered your butt plug
Blue-balled you forever
I am terrified
For what purports
To be the future
Neutered
Splayed open
A sink hole of regret
An exit strategy
Poorly executed
Long lost holiday
On ice
The world's now a
Shell shocked place
I am **so** not your miracle

People think I help
I hurt
I hurt everyone
Even animals
My gracious
Sociopath self

You are forever gone
You are your own
Exit strategy
Blindfolded
Poetics have killed millions

I am as good as road kill
Facing its demise
Eyes wide open

I just need to stop
Wanting to wash dishes
Instead of doing this

Gender has left the building
But I still inhabit
The problematics of mine

I didn't know
What being alone meant
Until I met you

Without chemistry
Or desire
Where do I leave this outfit?

Occupational hazard, sorry
My grinding brain
Goes grinding on

It's a fever pitched life
for us
It's a fever pitched
Life for us!

It was the worst of times
And it was the worst of times
On this device
It reads like a swan song

Who will pay for me?
Riding out over the holiday graves
Weathering myself
Because later there's supposed to be
A happy ending
Like in
DEYRKIMY
OWERLBIL
RYTENTH
PTRFARMES
LOVECO
CO*

* Dear Kim you will be alright in the performance Love coco

Wait! That was Wife 1
Wife 2 isn't supposed to care
Bewildered by your fall guy girlfriend
Who is too old to see

I'm watching you
Spring eternal
Squirming and struggling
And parlons-nous-ing yourself

This is the first time
I've ever been fully wholly
Alone in the void

Why can't I question it?
Well, I am now
At all your expenses
Because you've been what you've been yesterday
And Each begets Each

thank you
for always being so
supportive of me
letting me walk
into the void
holding your hand

poetry
is the best void for loneliness
don't you agree?

good evening

thank you for joining me again
in this interesting new
life testing
medium

I'm going to speak to you in an inaudible way

I hope this will relax you

up and around your ear and
deep down into your brain

back to front   front to back
side to side   side to side

okay   Okay   okay   okay

the sound of watchable breath

is now going to

woooooooosh out of the vortex for you

is that okay?

good

I'm on the other side now

sort of

now I'm going to use rough particles

they'll become my regularity
of
soft   spoken   personal   attention

today I just decided
to have some
one on one time with you

Is that okay?

I hope you trust me

you're very safe here with me

our existence as humans
is a constant struggle
we are here to experience lengthy good
and lengthy bad

let me tell you about a soft thud without a safety harness:

letting go of/

how I/

                                        control my/

/ body /

omnipotence
omnipotence

reverie
reverie

dread
dread

hate
hate

I'm so glad you're here with me
so I can softly whisper these words to you:
I like having you close

we are custodians of the past

knowing &

seeing &
not wanting to know

we're here together
just us

in the
/here & now/ &

in our

 /unknown/
future

          okay

  okay

                              okay

              okay

no memory
no desire
nothing

except my own

/perplexity/

the /brutal/
is not here

do you

wanna

 make the world

a better

place?

good!

a willow
deeply
                    scarred

somebody's
broken

                    heart
a washed-out

                                                        dream

washed

                              out

                         dream

follow the pattern

of the wind

that's why
I'm starting with me

starting with me

/I was mistaken/
I am going

D

O

W

N

watch my body

are you watching my body?

                                               good

my fear?

my excitement?

                                               good

my not knowing

what will happen?

do you like that?

good

my body

outside my mind

apart from gravity

I am now

Falling
fast

how are you?

good

did you hear my

thud?

                                                                    good

let's play that again

I'm now

upright
intentional
hungry with
directionality

okay

                                                    okay

okay

                                                            okay

then I let go
of how I can control

my body

good

you'll hear a roar
of psychic space
as it hits me

would you like to hear

the roar?

I'm going to softly
gently
give you
the roar

all around your head

and maybe
even in your ear
ready?

relax

you are safe here

get comfortable

I'm tucking you in
with a soft
heated silky
blanket

you are

loved

I

love

you

POW!

POW!

(500 millisecond pause)

VI

THE GREAT EMPTY GOODNIGHT

I am always forever never young again
And have gotten very good at #alt/alone
And it is my mission to tune-in to loneliness
And to feel it everywhere
In trees and plants and animals and in the human animal

Social conditions frame psychic ones
And face-plant one atop the other
A big fat pile-up of life and property distributions
Consensual curveballs
Melancholy on a budget
With parachuting capital accumulations
That alert us to the fact that it's so urban in here

I've now heard from a reputable source her feet are cut and bleeding
and she's running in the sand late and lost and dehydrated and too
naïve and I say:

That child is in a flood of phallic activity!

Ben: "K! Holy shit! I had a dream that you told me how to finish
editing my novel by saying: *remember that no matter how advanced
the characters' desires are, they are still just animals moving through
the world*.

It still means a lot to me
That I can make myself cum
The old fashioned way

The shit you smell
Just might be your own
The realest things seem poison
I'm ashamed to be a man

I'll show her a thing or two
That women don't know

My joy is in my mind
I don't need more of you there

Thought is sacred
Unlike us gross men

Technology took human emotion out of the world
(They know what they're doing)

I'll join the unruly rulers
The rulers who don't rule but rule those who rule those who rule

Ruling rulers rule!
You be quiet shhhhhhhhhhhhhhh

Can't you be happy?
It's a natural thing anyway

He brings the dreamer
A sad pig
A sad sow

I killed my father
I ate human flesh
And I quiver with joy

Freedom is an ordeal
You have to live through
Symbiotic, parasitic, and commensal

Earth takes back what it produces
Pigs take away evil and purify it
Perform miracles

She has herself buried
Beneath 20 meters of earth
She dies weeping
Her tears inundate the soil

Family is a body that donates itself
A last resort
Expressing feelings and
Making them candidates

Lots of detective work
Is worth the investment
To becoming aware
Of great things which are possible
Beyond recovery
Less safe than garments
Or découpaging a rare stamp
To a paperweight

Remember the gift
Must look good to the person
Who beats a path over and over again
Until it becomes home

Invention takes a toll
always has
that's the cruelest joke most of us know
what gets pinned on what
what passes the buck

Innovation takes a toll
(like being womanly)
goodnight menses
darkening wings of desire
history inside the volcano
of preservation management usage

Am I blue
in the field
of the iced-over crater?

Declared taxonomy of humanity
so-so humans
made-to-measure
in approximate length and width
of loving one another

Counter-volcanic axis of the feminine
and skin-envelopes of
the feminine
blown in from paradise

Is biography destiny's
dust-up with
skin, volume, shadow, light
and can the feminine carve the way
if invention takes a toll
by melting traces on molten ground
of our own poly-resin orbit
of who is speaking?

Fixed fugitive moments
Connecting ephemeral unconscious
to paths of no resistance
only burdens of proof
sculptural séance conditions
for a past as-yet-to-come

Intervening space is visiting ruins
and all love presumably left among them
presuming even the possibility of love
or a world that can repair
let the hating world be known
oh wait—it already is

I am 20 thousand leagues
under my epicenter
what forms me
is molten endurance
experience pressed
through my own skin
I'm able to recognize carnival gloss
for what it is
an heirloom
emptied out blood box for seeing
recycled water bottle of my own tears

Able to see history for what it is
a natural selection site
double-axis pirouette
of the feminine and the sculptural

Is biography destiny?
Are sculptural conditions required
for time-to-come
(avenir) intervenes space
mines objects mired within ruins
of pressed-down hate and love

During the dangerous campaign
and through a lot
of advantageous
and unrealizable conditions
an amorous arrow to the heart
fulfilled my ask

Yoked in fiery bulls
stuck with glue grown from them
put to sleep unsleeping
her father didn't give
a cause to carve his limbs
and throw them out to sea

Return youth!
let go old blood!
pour in new blood!

We are undone
light is to grief
as begging is to parity
paltry hiding places
remote nooks and crannies
of the realm of the
universe overwhelmed
and in ruins

Let all things pass
'cause no one may safely assail
the strong
cure's worse than the peril
or memory of my better self
my shitty fortunes
the throng of the silent
a little boy excited
by the moves of his stepmother
who water-feeds the flames
strange nuptials
follow up face attacks so well begun
grief is just practicum
so glad I armed my daughter

Horror smites my heart
the mother has come back
the wife is banished
a way through has opened for me

I cannot believe I'm becoming a mountain of repeat
I don't believe in that mountain
and now I made it
I paid homage too late
I messed with my ancestors
I let the void fuck me up

We are babies, boats, and roses
A multiverse of pleasure annihilation
a perpetual going-on-being of utopias
like my mother making noodles
until her skin falls off
her debt to nature and the natural world
something to offer the bars of my jail

I feel a day old plus more
in my house and in my chores
but also know to say what I must
my aims are involuntary
I can see in the dark
into the "truth" of everything we know

Cultural infiltrations and even the process of thinking itself
an elaboration of what cannot be fully mapped
when we have to say a goodbye
so thick you could bite it
death in a universalizing storm
absence as a condition of thinking
that was my child
on the rails pulling out
into the darkness

What is required to come to life?
is form the performance?
is contact at odds with delivering
these opposites
which are so much everywhere
my personality statues
my barbaric natural body's way to consolidate
a careful commodity that is not containing anything
that is not a vessel for anything
but a sensory smatter of self-hood some people never get together
as in what does it mean that I can't take a lifetime
in this aggravating acceleration
to say
what I
must

THE OTTOLINE PRIZE

Tina Brown Celona   *The Real Moon of Poetry*
& Other Poems

Rosemary Griggs   *Sky Girl*
Harmony Holiday   *Negro League Baseball*
Lesle Lewis   *Rainy Days on the Farm*
Kaisa Ullsvik Miller   *Unspoiled Air*
Chelsey Minnis   *Zirconia*
Lauren Shufran   *Inter Arma*
Josie Sigler   *Living Must Bury*
Laura Sims   *Practice, Restraint*
Ariana Reines   *The Cow*
Beth Roberts   *Like You*
Sasha Steensen   *A Magic Book*
Stacy Szymaszek   *Journal of Ugly Sites*
and Other Journals

Wendy Xu   *Phrasis*
Elizabeth Marie Young   *Aim Straight at the Fountain*
and Press Vaporize

ACKNOWLEDGMENTS

Parts of chapter VI appeared in performance with Shiv Kotecha at Codex bookstore, NYC, 2019 and online in *Gauss PDF*, 2019.

A version of chapter VI was performed at Art Cake, NYC in conjunction with Suzanne Bocanegra's *Wardrobe Test*, 2019.

Thank you to the intrepid editors of the following publications for first amplifying the earliest versions of these poems: *Panda's Friend, Newest York, Parallax: Poetic Visions* (Hauser & Wirth), *Alignment 3* (American Medium), *Gauss PDF,* and *A Plume Annual* Volume 1.

Heartfelt thanks to Joseph Mosconi for immediate enthusiasm for this manuscript, and to Matvei Yankelevich who has supported my work for decades. Without his generous editorial humanity and personal grace, too much important work would not exist.

Shiv Kotecha, Mónica de la Torre, Lucy Ives, Steven Zultanski, Joey Yearous-Algozin, Trisha Low, Holly Melgard, and Aaron Winslow tended carefully to this manuscript while it was still a tadpole, offering insight, challenging questions, plenty of laughs, and wise council that seeded this book's growth.

Full fathom five thanks to Fence Books; Founding Editor Rebecca Wolff, (I am grateful that *Phantom Captain* slipped in under the wire to be her last edited Fence book) and Editorial Co-Directors Emily Wallis Hughes, Jason Zuzga, and Benefactress Jennifer S. Epstein for choosing this peculiar book, and for their care, excitement, endowment, and sheer hard work in guiding *Phantom Captain* into open waters.

I am thankful for the life-lines and anchors provided by friends, family (especially Coco Fitterman Rob Fitterman and Lenù), mentors, patients, colleagues, independent bookstores, independent presses, and independent thinking.

FENCE BOOKS

Dear Kim,

I have read and experienced with fascination this Universe you have written. I have found both a chrysographic and quixotic quest for what this book writhes under the reader's punctuated paths:

a) broken table for my thalassic friend: here begins the reading of the book, not for the faint of heartbeat but rather transplanting accounts of a grimoire that takes one further turn onward with hard-khora tidbits . . .

b) or should you say us reading caressing the hand when breathing tho' injur'd Thales, if the step toward environ-mental constellation of our shared lexicographical sculpting weaves in its rooted figuræ water meeting fire.

I have met the unruly captain's infinite grace in the marriage of my agnomia and logorrhea; it blows out: is the thunder between the hyper-chaotic marriage of flexible arrows expounding in nomenclatural autopsy?

—standing timorous in front of the cataphract of the undifferentiated you-you-you a third meaning of a shell—this book is three-way street revocation of the edict of Klassics, of the book that should be rather something that for the best of us could be a manual amicorum, or more than anything a kiss-analysis of the buck spliced to your eyes, in ink when ink is bookishly sculpted and excavated.

I followed with pure devotion of such an invitation to an imminent realm bearing the gift of an orangy-red alchimery.

I truly want to keep thinking this through and exploring more. I'm mesmerized by the perambulations, foldings, and permutations that this book-object/installation/performance takes. As if the reader is giving form to the book while the author is writing from the most distant angle of a lateral vision in sculpture, in forming a distracted captain.

This is the kind of book I needed to read and also the kind of book I want to write.   FREDERICK ARIAS

Exuberant and emotional, playfully and plaintively raging, disruptive, ribald, and Rabelaisian polyvocal philosophical machinations, a performance that collapses corporeal boundaries in a collective post Anthropocene space where *Alles hat ein Ende nur die Wurst hat zwei* = **Everything has one end, only the sausage has two**. *Phantom Captain* contains multitudes.
                                         ERICA BAUM

in·ef·fa·ble
The only word to describe the experience of reading *Phantom Captain*. Kim takes you on a journey that is familiar, strange, unknowing and thrilling.
                              STEVEN COX & DANIEL SILVER

In *Phantom Captain*, Kim Rosenfield is at the top of her game. These poems make me feel uneasy. They churn with efforts at sense-making that always fall apart. They give me that swervy feeling you get when a car hits a bump in the road that's more like a mini-ramp and your tummy goes wooosh with the precipitous dip back to earth. The bounce of physics, but emotionally, the language of that; psychological whiplash; finding your associations false; thinking with the shredding environment; the texture of panic; the fantasy of animal equilibrium; the joke of trying to make oneself whole in a culture of ephemeralization; affect as wind pattern; the gross hilarity of aging; the defensiveness of trying not to die. From the shadowy caverns of human experience, something that defies direct description emerges here through Rosenfield's adept elisions, wild logics, and brilliant, catastrophic failures to make it all make sense.

KRISTEN GALLAGHER

Phantom Captain charts an archipelago of language in the ocean of unnamed emotional life by playfully collaging together aphoristic metaphors, quotidian expressions of phrase, phenomenology, and psychoanalysis with daringly bald lyric address. In these "intersubjective processes between subject and biographer," "mate" and "captain," herein, the voice of the poem emerges out of the rigorous labor of unfurling knowing's certainty.

HOLLY MELGARD

When Kim Rosenfield writes that she wants "the ineffable experience of the limitless infinite and the unthought known and forms of not knowing," she says so in a voice that threads between all the known shades of affect. It's a singer's voice, intimate and impersonal, vibing on epistemology, Nietzsche, and the most gloriously fecund perfume ever conjured in prose. A thrilling and contrarian read.

MARINA ROSENFELD

In *Phantom Captain*, Kim Rosenfield reminds the reader that even in the worst of times, our broken vessels, battered by waves and taking on water without safe harbor in sight, somehow manage to continue on. Driven compulsively forward, through a dazzling array of poetic forms, the many voices of her poems brave this vast ocean as they struggle to establish connection with the outside and fight against the inevitable and final transformation into a dead object floating out there, away from shore.

JOEY YEAROUS-ALGOZIN